KEEPSAKES

DREAMS

CLB 4396
Published 1995 by CLB Publishing
Exclusively for Selectabook Ltd, Devizes
© 1995 CLB Publishing, Godalming, Surrey
ISBN 1-85833-297-4

Printed in Hong Kong by Imago

KEEPSAKES

DREAMS

Compiled by
Betty Sullivan

SELECT
EDITIONS

Joseph's Dream

OSEPH HAD A dream, and when he told it to his brothers, they hated him all the more. He said to them, 'Listen to this dream I had. We were binding sheaves of corn out in the field when suddenly my sheaf rose and stood upright, while your sheaves gathered round mine and bowed down to it.' His brothers said to him, 'Do you intend to reign over us? Will you actually rule us?' And they hated him all the more because of his dream and what he had said.

Then he had another dream, and he told it to his brothers. 'Listen,' he said, 'I had another dream, and this time the sun and moon and eleven stars were bowing down to me.' When he told his father as well as his brothers, his father rebuked him and said, 'What is this dream you had? Will your mother and I and your brothers actually come and bow down to the ground before you?' His brothers were jealous of him, but his father kept the matter in mind.

HOLY BIBLE, NEW INTERNATIONAL VERSION. GENESIS 37:5-11

Sweet Dreams

My eyes make pictures when they are shut;
   I see a fountain, large and fair,
A willow and a ruined hut,
   And thee, and me and Mary there.
O Mary! make thy gentle lap our pillow!
Bend o'er us, like a bower, my beautiful green willow!

SAMUEL TAYLOR COLERIDGE

I arise from dreams of thee
   In the first sweet sleep of night,
When the winds are breathing low
   And the stars are shining bright.

PERCY BYSSHE SHELLEY

It was a dream of perfect bliss, too beautiful to last.

T. H. BAYLY

Island of Dreams

My dream is of an island place
   Which distant seas keep lonely;
A little island, on whose face
   The stars are watchers only.
Those bright still stars! they need not seem
Brighter or stiller in my dream.

An island full of hills and dells,
   All rumpled and uneven
With green recesses, sudden swells,
   And odorous valleys driven
So deep and straight, that always there
The wind is cradled to soft air.

Hills running up to heaven for light
   Through woods that half-way ran!
As if the wild earth mimicked right
   The wilder heart of man:
Only it shall be greener far
And gladder than hearts ever are.

HENRY WADSWORTH LONGFELLOW

The Emperor Claims his Bride

NE DAY A Roman emperor called Macsen Wledig went hunting long ago with his attendants. After a while, because of the heat, he decided to lie down and take a short rest. There in the warmth he fell asleep and began to dream. He was now in a river valley and saw ahead of him a mountain that seemed as high as the top of the sky. He crossed the mountain and then a broad plain with majestic rivers flowing to the sea. At the mouth of one of the rivers was a large city that had a castle with coloured towers. On the river rode a huge fleet of ships. One particular vessel stood out from the rest, having gold and silver planks. Macsen boarded it and set sail, eventually reaching the most beautiful island he had ever seen. He crossed this land and came upon a rugged country of valleys and hills, unlike anything he had ever known. He saw a mountain, a river flowing to the sea, and a castle adorned with gold and silver. He entered the castle and saw two red-haired youths playing a board-game. Nearby was a grey-haired veteran. Macsen then saw a maiden dressed in white silk seated on a golden chair. She was exceptionally beautiful. She rose to greet Macsen, who embraced her, whereupon Macsen awoke from his dream.

He returned to Rome, but he yearned to see again the beauty he had dreamed about. Messengers were sent to find her, but they failed. Then the emperor's chief adviser suggested he follow the route he took that day he went hunting, and Macsen did so. When he reached the spot where he had rested he told his messengers to travel westwards, as he had done in his dream. This they did, and they soon came upon a huge mountain, crossed a broad plain and followed a river to its mouth on the sea where they found a large city in which stood a castle with coloured towers. They saw a huge fleet of ships and boarded the most spectacular vessel. They set sail . . . . They saw a mountain, a river and a castle at its mouth. They entered the castle and saw the two youths Macsen had told them about, and the old man, and there, in a golden chair, a maiden of utmost beauty. The messengers told the maiden of the emperor's love for her. 'If he loves me, let him come to me,' she said. And so the messengers returned to Rome and told Macsen the good news.

Without delay the emperor mounted his horse and set out on his journey, guided by the messengers. At length they reached the land of hills and valleys, and the castle, which they entered. There still were the red-haired youths, the old man, and the beautiful maiden of Macsen's dream. The emperor knelt down and paid homage to her as Empress of Rome. And so Macsen Wledig claimed his bride.

WELSH LEGEND

Kubla Khan

In Xanadu did Kubla Khan
   A stately pleasure-dome decree,
Where Alph, the sacred river, ran
   Through caverns measureless to man
Down to a sunless sea.
   So twice five miles of fertile ground
With walls and towers were girdled round.
   And there were gardens bright with sinuous rills,
Where blossomed many an incense-bearing tree.
   And here were forests ancient as the hills,
Enfolding sunny spots of greenery.

But oh! that deep romantic chasm which slanted
   Down the green hill athwart a cedarn cover!
A savage place! as holy and enchanted
   As e'er beneath a waning moon was haunted
By woman wailing for her demon-lover!
   And from this chasm, with ceaseless turmoil seething,
As if this earth in fast thick pants were breathing,
   A mighty fountain momently was forced,
Amid whose swift half-intermitted burst
   Huge fragments vaulted like rebounding hail,
Or chaffy grain beneath the thresher's flail.

SAMUEL TAYLOR COLERIDGE

Dreams of Bliss

I love the silent hour of night,
    For blissful dreams may then arise,
Revealing to my charmed sight
    What may not bless my waking eyes.

And then a voice may meet my ear,
    That death has silenced long ago;
And hope and rapture may appear
    Instead of solitude and woe.

Cold in the grave for years has lain
    The form it was my bliss to see;
And only dreams can bring again
    The darling of my heart to me.

ANNE BRONTE

I've pondered life and it's nothing but a dream.
Our tears and laughter are dreams within dreams.
So be it. What else can we do but enjoy this dream of life?

CHU UI-SHIK

Land of Dreams

Awake, awake, my little Boy!
   Thou wast thy Mother's only joy:
Why dost thou weep in thy gentle sleep?
   Awake! thy Father does thee keep.

'O, what land is the Land of Dreams,
   What are its mountains, and what are its streams?
O Father! I saw my Mother there,
   Among the Lillies by waters fair.

'Among the lambs clothèd in white,
   She walked with her Thomas in sweet delight.
I wept for joy, like a dove I mourn;
   O! when shall I again return?'

Dear Child, I also by pleasant streams
   Have wandered all night in the Land of Dreams,
But tho' calm and warm the waters wide,
   I could not get to the other side.

'Father, O Father! what do we here,
   In this Land of unbelief and fear?
The Land of Dreams is better far
   Above the light of the Morning Star.'

WILLIAM BLAKE

The Dream Fairy

A little fairy comes at night,
   Her eyes are blue, her hair is brown,
With silver spots upon her wings,
   And from the moon she flutters down.

She has a little silver wand,
   And when a good child goes to bed
She waves her wand from right to left
   And makes a circle round her head.

And then it dreams of pleasant things,
   Of fountains filled with fairy fish,
And trees that bear delicious fruit,
   And bow their branches at a wish;

Of arbours filled with dainty scents
   From lovely flowers that never fade,
Bright flies that glitter in the sun,
   And glow-worms shining in the shade;

And talking birds with gifted tongues
   For singing songs and telling tales,
And pretty dwarfs to show the way
   Through fairy hills and fairy dales.

THOMAS HOOD

Bounteous Vision

Methought I stood where trees of every clime,
    Palm, myrtle, oak, and sycamore, and beech,
With plantain, and spice-blossoms, made a screen;
    In neighbourhood of fountains (by the noise
Soft-showering in my ears), and, (by the touch
    Of scent,) not far from roses. Turning round
I saw an arbour with a drooping roof
    Of trellis vines, and bells, and larger blooms,
Like floral censers, swinging light in air;
    Before its wreathed doorway, on a mound
Of moss, was spread a feast of summer fruits,
    Which, nearer seen, seem'd refuse of a meal
By angel tasted or our Mother Eve;
    For empty shells were scattered on the grass,
And grape-stalks but half bare, and remnants more,
    Sweet-smelling, whose pure kinds I could not know.

JOHN KEATS

Rabbit in a Hurry

ALICE WAS beginning to get very tired of sitting by her sister on the bank, and of having nothing to do.... So she was considering in her own mind (as well as she could, for the hot day made her feel very sleepy and stupid), whether the pleasure of making a daisy-chain would be worth the trouble of getting up and picking the daisies, when suddenly a White Rabbit with pink eyes ran close by her.

There was nothing so *very* remarkable in that: nor did Alice think it so *very* much out of the way to hear the Rabbit say to itself, 'Oh dear! Oh dear! I shall be too late!' (when she thought it over afterwards, it occurred to her that she ought to have wondered at this, but at the time it all seemed quite natural); but when the Rabbit actually *took a watch out of its waistcoat-pocket*, and looked at it, and then hurried on, Alice started to her feet, for it flashed across her mind that she had never before seen a rabbit with either a waistcoat-pocket or a watch to take out of it, and burning with curiosity, she ran across the field after it, and was just in time to see it pop down a large rabbit-hole under the hedge.

LEWIS CARROLL

Hail Emily

At length, into the obscure Forest came
    The Vision I had sought through grief and shame.
Athwart that wintry wilderness of thorns
    Flashed from her motion splendour like the Morn's,
And from her presence life was radiated
    Through the gray earth and branches bare and dead;
So that her way was paved, and roofed above
    With flowers as soft as thoughts of budding love;
And odours warm and fresh fell from her hair
    Dissolving the dull cold in the frore air:
Soft as an Incarnation of the Sun,
    When light is changed to love, this glorious One
Floated into the cavern where I lay,
    And called my Spirit, and the dreaming clay
Was lifted by the thing that dreamed below
    As smoke by fire, and in her beauty's glow
I stood, and felt the dawn of my long night
    Was penetrating me with living light:
I knew it was the Vision veiled from me
    So many years – that it was Emily.

PERCY BYSSHE SHELLEY

Dream-Pedlary

If there were dreams to sell,
  What would you buy?
Some cost a passing bell;
  Some a light sigh,
That shakes from Life's fresh crown
Only a rose-leaf down.
If there were dreams to sell,
Merry and sad to tell,
And the crier rung the bell,
  What would you buy?

A cottage lone and still,
  With bowers nigh,
Shadowy, my woes to still,
  Until I die.
Such pearl from Life's fresh crown
Fain would I shake me down.
Were dreams to have at will,
This would best heal my ill,
  This would I buy.

THOMAS LOVELL BEDDOES

Utter Rot!

OWING AND CUMMINGS had dropped in during the evening, and I suddenly remembered an extraordinary dream I had a few nights ago, and I thought I would tell them about it. I dreamt I saw some huge blocks of ice in a shop with a bright glare behind them. I walked into the shop and the heat was overpowering. I found that the blocks of ice were on fire. The whole thing was so real and so supernatural I woke up in a cold perspiration. Lupin in a most contemptuous manner, said: 'What utter rot!'

Before I could reply, Gowing said there was nothing so completely uninteresting as other people's dreams.

I appealed to Cummings, but he said he was bound to agree with the others, and my dream was especially nonsensical. I said: 'It seemed so real to me.' Gowing replied: 'Yes, to *you*, perhaps, but not to *us*.' Whereupon they all roared.

Carrie, who had hitherto been quiet, said: 'He tells me his stupid dreams every morning nearly.' I replied: 'Very well, dear, I promise you I will never tell you or anybody else another dream of mine the longest day I live.' Lupin said: 'Hear! hear!' and helped himself to another glass of beer.

GEORGE AND WEEDON GROSSMITH

Stairway to Heaven

ACOB LEFT Beersheba and set out for Haran. When he reached a certain place he stopped for the night because the sun had set. Taking one of the stones there, he put it under his head and lay down to sleep. He had a dream in which he saw a stairway resting on the earth, with its top reaching to heaven, and the angels of God were ascending and descending on it. There above it stood the Lord, and he said: 'I am the Lord, the God of your father Abraham and the God of Isaac. I will give you and your descendants the land on which you are lying. Your descendants will be like the dust of the earth, and you will spread out to the west and to the east, to the north and to the south. All peoples on earth will be blessed through you and your offspring. I am with you and will watch over you wherever you go, and I will bring you back to this land. I will not leave you until I have done what I have promised you.'

When Jacob awoke from his sleep he thought, 'Surely the Lord is in this place, and I was not aware of it.' He was afraid and said, 'How awesome is this place! This is none other than the house of God; this is the gate of heaven.'

HOLY BIBLE, NEW INTERNATIONAL VERSION. GENESIS 28:10-17

begunde: der heilige patriarche. des wir
berot starche. allez sin geslæhte. als er vil
wol mahte. sie wrden des gefröwet. daz
er was bescowet: von gotes anblike. si suh
ten vene dicke: gegen den himilisgen cho
ren. hie muget ir wnder horen.

Gula Jarob

Innocent Night

I dream'd we both were in a bed
    Of Roses, almost smotherèd:
The warmth and sweetnes had me there
    Made lovingly familiar;
But that I heard thy sweet breath say,
    Faults done by night, will blush by day:
I kist thee (panting), and I call
    Night to the Record! that was all.
But ah! if empty dreames so please,
    Love, give me more such nights as these.

Me thought (last night) Love in an anger came,
    And brought a rod, so whipt me with the same:
Mirtle the twigs were, meerly to imply,
    Love strikes, but 'tis with gentle crueltie.
Patient I was: Love pitifull grew then,
    And stroak'd the stripes, and I was whole agen.
Thus like a Bee, Love-gentle stil doth bring
    Hony to salve, where he before did sting.

ROBERT HERRICK

Bright Be Thy Dreams!

Bright be thy dreams – may all thy weeping
Turn into smiles while thou art sleeping:
    Those by death or seas removed,
  Friends, who in thy spring-time knew thee,
    All thou'st ever prized or loved,
  In dreams come smiling to thee!

There may the child, whose love lay deepest,
Dearest of all, come while thou sleepest:
    Still the same – no charm forgot–
  Nothing lost that life had given;
    Or, if changed, but changed to what
  Thou'lt find her yet in Heaven!

THOMAS MOORE

With You in Sleep

Had I but two little wings,
    And were a little feathery bird,
To you I'd fly, my dear,
    But thoughts like these are idle things,
And I stay here.

But in my sleep to you I fly,
    I'm always with you in my sleep,
The world is all one's own,
    But then one wakes and where am I?
All, all alone.

Sleep stays not though a monarch bids,
    So I love to wake at break of day,
For though my sleep be gone,
    Yet while 'tis dark one shuts one's lids,
And so, dreams on.

KATHERINE MANSFIELD

Dream Within a Dream

Take this kiss upon the brow!
   And, in parting from you now,
Thus much let me avow –
   You are not wrong, who deem
That my days have been a dream:
   Yet if hope has flown away
In a night, or in a day,
   In a vision, or in none,
Is it therefore the less *gone*?
   All that we see or seem
Is but a dream within a dream.

I stand amid the roar
   Of a surf-tormented shore,
And I hold within my hand
   Grains of the golden sand –
How few! yet how they creep
   Through my fingers to the deep,
While I weep – while I weep!
   O God! can I not save
One from the pitiless wave?
   Is *all* that we see or seem
But a dream within a dream?

EDGAR ALLAN POE

The Magic Land

At seven, when I go to bed,
   I find such pictures in my head:
Castles with dragons prowling round,
   Gardens where magic fruits are found;
Fair ladies prisoned in a tower,
   Or lost in an enchanted bower,
While gallant horsemen ride by streams
   That border all this land of dreams
I find, so clearly in my head
   At seven, when I go to bed.

At seven, when I wake again,
   The magic land I seek in vain;
A chair stands where the castle frowned,
   The carpet hides the garden ground,
No fairies trip across the floor,
   Boots, and not horsemen, flank the door,
And where the blue streams rippling ran
   Is now a bath and water-can;
I seek the magic land in vain
   At seven, when I wake again.

ROBERT LOUIS STEVENSON

Sources and Acknowledgments

For permission to reproduce illustrations, the publishers thank the following: Mary Evans Picture Library, E. T. Archive, Manchester City Art Galleries, Victoria and Albert Museum London, the Mansell Collection and Sam Elder.